PORSCHE

PORSCHE

MICHAEL COTTON

Designed by
PHILIP CLUCAS MSIAD

Produced by
TED SMART and **DAVID GIBBON**

CRESCENT BOOKS
NEW YORK

FOREWORD

I am, in all modesty, delighted to be associated with the tribute that this book must pay to Professor Porsche, who in my family has always been looked upon as the Albert Einstein of automobile engineering. Indeed we believe that he holds that position 'de facto' in the history of motor engineering and achievement, and I am often astonished that the parallel between these two scientists is not more frequently drawn because it is obvious that those who write about such things secretly share my conviction.

In trying to recapture in a few lines the experiences I have had in the course of my life and my career of the name Porsche and the cars which bear its mark, I am compelled to start with a few personal memories even if they are without any particular historical significance, so I ask you to bear with me!

They go back to 1955 to be exact. I was ten years old and Porsche, which had only just been born as a make of car, already represented a secret dream of mine. I had the pleasure of accompanying my father in a bright red Carrera 1500 on a marvellous journey of over seven hundred kilometres, from the factory to the Geneva show. My father, who only a short time previously had won the Liège-Rome-Liège race, was certainly the ideal man to show me just how finely tuned that extraordinary car was and how well suited it was to an expert driver.

My next encounter with Porsche was some years later with the prestigious 908 three litre model of 1968. By that time it had become a formidable rival to the Ford Mirage and John Wyer's G.T.40 that I was driving.

I often had the opportunity for a close look, and when the 908 evolved into the 917 in 1970 and 1971, in the days of the Ferrari 512, I must admit that in the nicest possible way I had occasion to envy my friends Siffert and Rodriguez, who were achieving amazingly spectacular things behind their wheels.

One or two generations of racing Porsches later, I had the great satisfaction of being able to work with that most impressive team of engineers, who for years had been contributing in a very decisive way to the shape of the cars of tomorrow – men capable, for example, of putting together the parts for a new winning racing car in the space of three months.

Do not let us forget that from the technical point of view Porsche is so advanced that recently, in 1976, the competitors and the organisers of the Can-am did everything they could to prevent them from continuing to take part in their races or that similarly, in 1979, a lobby at Indianapolis managed to get the rules changed at the very last minute just to stop Porsche coming to upset their plans!

It was precisely the same engine, originally intended for Indianapolis, which enabled me and my companion Derek Bell to take the Le Mans 24 hour race in 1981, despite the fact that this powerful piece of machinery had never been tested in a race. Doubtless this was simply further striking evidence of the reliability of those exceptional engines.

The history of the house of Porsche is not one for those who subscribe to convention; the cars that bear its name are decidedly different from any others. No doubt this will always be the case for as long as there are Porsches, for behind the Porsche cars lies an extremely powerful technological world, imbued with a wealth of knowledge and generating inventive resources which are probably unique.

JACKY ICKX

Old and new. The 911 Turbo (above) is a direct descendent of the 2-litre, 130 horsepower 911 that made its debut in 1963 — but now the engine is enlarged to 3.3 litres for the most expensive model in the range, and develops 300 horsepower. The 944 (left) is the shape of the future....

PORSCHE—THE INVENTOR

Professor Ferdinand Porsche, born in 1875, was one of the world's most prolific and renowned motoring inventors. His early interest in electricity led to two electric hub-driven motor cars at the turn of the century, the chassis being Lohner. In 1931 Porsche opened his own design consultancy in Stuttgart and one of his first commissions

was for the Auto-Union Grand Prix car which, along with the rival Mercedes design, made Germany's silver racing cars almost invincible in the pre-war era. Simplicity of design was always a prime requirement, and this was carried over to the RS Spyder (below left) in 1959.

First and foremost, Professor Ferdinand Porsche was an inventor. His early passion was electrical engineering and in 1890, at the age of 15, Ferdinand had an argument with his father that might be repeated in many households containing teenage children. Not that it was a typical family row; it came about because Ferdinand wanted to design and install electric lighting in the home. At the time there was no electricity in Maffersdorf, a village in the northern part of Bohemia, and Porsche senior sternly forbade the experiment—he wanted Ferdinand to concentrate on the family craft of tinsmith. Ferdinand persisted, however, with the tacit support of his mother, in building a generator, switchboard, wiring and everything else, and to the great amazement of all the neighbours, the Porsche home was eventually lit by electricity. A few days later the owner of a local factory persuaded Anton Porsche that his son should attend the Technical University in Vienna, and at the age of 18, Ferdinand's career began to take shape.

Ferdinand Porsche's studies were supported by Bela Egger, an electrical company that later became Brown Boveri, and after four years he became manager of the company's test department. In 1898 Porsche was approached by Jacob Lohner, a famous Austrian carriage maker, and accepted an offer to join his company to produce a motor car that was to be the sensation of the Paris Salon in 1900. The Lohner-Porsche

had an electrically powered hub motor in each wheel, each producing 2.5 horsepower, enabling the car to reach a swift and silent maximum speed of 37 kph. The design principles of this car were to be incorporated in the American moon buggy three-quarters of a century later!

Ferdinand Porsche—inventor, designer, automobile engineer and racing driver—was appointed technical director of the Austro-Daimler company in 1905, at the age of 30. Road cars, commercial vehicles, racing cars, aero engines and airship motors were all part of his work, and the advent of war in 1914 added a new dimension. The so-called 'land train' was evolved by Porsche to transport heavy guns and other military paraphernalia across any terrain, still relying on a 'mixte' hub driven series of motors. Examples of this invention are still to be seen where vast loads have to be moved. In 1916 Porsche, now the managing director of Austro-Daimler, was awarded the Officer's Cross of the Franz Joseph medal, and an honorary doctorate by the University of Vienna.

In the immediate postwar years Porsche designed Austria's small car, the Sascha, a small four-cylinder engine vehicle of 2-litre capacity. With his innate love of motor racing, Porsche designed the prototype as a racing car and three of these were entered in the Targa Florio race in

1922, pitched against far larger and more powerful machines. The best placed Sascha, at the hands of the legendary Alfred Neubauer, finished in seventh place, an easy class winner. But by now Porsche's penchant for competitions was causing arguments in the boardroom, and by the time the Sascha appeared in road trim in 1923, Porsche had moved on to a new position as technical director and board member of Daimler-Benz in Stuttgart.

SSKL supercharged models scored dozens of racing and hillclimb successes, whilst the related road cars became the epitome of fast luxury motoring in Europe.

Even this was not enough to satisfy Porsche, by now acknowledged in his own time as a genius. His quick temper, and inability to compromise, led to friction and by 1929 he was ready to move on again, this time returning to his native Austria to join the board of the Steyr

Porsche was the first designer to put the engine into the rear of a successful racing car. Although the Auto-Union, (6) which bristled with innovative features such as torsion bar suspension, (8) was deemed difficult to drive it was, perhaps, the drivers who needed to adapt to its characteristics. (7) Two generations of Porsche design: the supercharged Auto-Union, and the turbocharged 924 Carrera GT and the racing derivative.

Never afraid to get his hands dirty, Porsche reversed the autocratic trend, solving many problems by crawling under the cars to see for himself what was causing the trouble. His first brief was to develop a 2-litre supercharged racing car for Daimler-Benz, and this was accomplished to such effect that in 1924 Christian Werner triumphed in the tough Sicilian event, to the joy of the German nation. Porsche was awarded his second honorary doctorate by the University of Stuttgart.

In five and a half years Porsche designed a whole family of road and racing cars for Daimler-Benz, all of which are regarded today as classics and worth fabulous sums of money. In particular the S, SS, SSK and

company. Immediately he set to work updating the firm's XXX model and designing an advanced new car called the 'Austria', powered by an eight cylinder, 5.3 litre engine. This model, featuring swing axles, made its debut at the Paris Salon that autumn, but Porsche's return to Austria was marred by the closure of Steyr's bank, later to be taken over by the 'Creditanstalt am Hof' bank which handled Austro-Daimler's business, and predictably, the Steyr company was soon merged with Austro-Daimler, from whom Porsche had parted on less than cordial terms seven years earlier.

Now Porsche had to plan his next move, and it was almost

THE DESIGN CONSULTANCY

1   2

inevitable that he should choose to set up his own design consultancy in Stuttgart. He installed himself and a small team, headed by chief engineer Karl Rabe, in a small office in Kronenstrasse.

Dr. Ing. h.c. Ferdinand Porsche GmbH was incorporated in January 1931, the company already having its first commission; to design a family car for the Wanderer concern. Porsche astutely decided to number his first design '7' so that it should not appear to the outside world that he was experimenting! The Wanderer featured a light alloy six cylinder engine with capacities of 1,700 cc, 1,860 cc or 2,000 cc, and swing axle rear suspension. It proved a popular design, to be followed by a larger model designed by Porsche with an eight cylinder engine, though the type 8 never went beyond the prototype stage.

A contract for a small, rear-engined passenger car followed from the Zündapp Works, noted at the time for its motorcycles. Porsche proposed an air-cooled, flat-four engine, but Zündapp wanted a five-cylinder water cooled radial design, which he subsequently created.

Now Porsche was wooed by the Russian government, who offered him the post of "State Designer of Russia" if he would take charge of industrial development in the Communist state.

For many men this challenge would have been impossible to refuse, but Porsche was eager to further his interest in motor-sport, an area lacking in opportunity in Russia.

Instead, Chancellor Adolf Hitler called Porsche to Berlin and asked him to build a people's car which would sell for under 1,000 marks—an impossibly low price, but Porsche was prepared to try. His type 60 design, revealed in January 1934, was for an aerodynamically styled four seater car which had an air-cooled engine at the rear. Predictably, recalling the Zündapp episode, the model would have a flat-four engine behind the gearbox, and would employ swing axle suspension.

It took two more years for the first three prototypes to be put through their paces, to be followed in 1937 by a further series of 30 prototypes built to Porsche's design in the Daimler-Benz works. It was apparent to realists that the price couldn't be reduced below 1,500 marks

without a government subsidy, but when in 1938 the government invited the public to pay advance subscriptions for ownership of the Volkswagen, a price of 990 marks was announced.

What of motor racing, though? Porsche had foreseen the new Grand Prix racing formula limiting cars to a maximum weight of 750 kilogrammes, which was to come in 1934, and had drawn his preliminary designs two years earlier. Designs for the Porsche type 22 Grand Prix car just happened to be handy when the directors of Auto-Union were visiting, and since they were of like mind, no time was lost in concluding a deal—Porsche's radical 16-cylinder racing car, with its engine *behind* the driver, would be built by Auto-Union. State assistance was received for this and the rival Daimler-Benz Grand Prix car, with the avowed intention of putting Germany at the forefront of world class motor racing. In this, the German industry was overwhelmingly successful through the years 1934 to 1939, establishing almost complete dominance over the Italian, French and British racing teams. By the time war broke out, Porsche was a giant among automotive designers—whilst still heading a small consultancy in an independent studio.

Porsche's son, Ferdinand "Ferry" Porsche, played an increasingly important part in the team during the 1930s. Like his father he loved motor racing, and was the first test driver for the Auto-Union P-wagen. Trained as an engineer, Ferry assisted in a great variety of designs, including tractors, and even in the planning of the Wolfsburg plant in which Volkswagens were to be produced. In 1939 Porsche senior was awarded a State Professorship in recognition of his services, which took a new turn in wartime conditions. Military versions of the Volkswagen, including amphibious and desert conversions, guns, tanks (including the Tiger and the 'Maus', at 188 tons the largest the world has ever seen) and aero engines, were all developed by the Porsche team.

In 1944 Porsche and his team were moved to Gmünd, in Austria, to continue their work in greater safety, and there they remained until the war was over. At 70, Professor Porsche's work was nearly done.

The Porsche family, virtually exiled in Austria, was not exempted from the the trials and tribulations that followed the war. Professor Porsche, his brother-in-law Dr. Anton Piëch, and Ferry Porsche were all detained by the Allies for questioning, followed by a period of internment; Prof. Porsche having to spend almost two years in the hands of the French, assisting with the design of the Renault 4CV. Ferry was the first to be released, immediately putting all his energy into piecing together the remnants of the Porsche design business.

Repairing Volkswagen cars just about paid the rent at Gmünd, and the first new design from the firm's drawing boards was for a twin cylinder air-cooled tractor; the second was a technically advanced Cisitalia Grand Prix car with four-wheel drive, commissioned by the Italian Piero Dusio, the fee for this project paying for Prof. Porsche's release from the French in August 1947.

Plans for the 356 sports car, the first model to bear Porsche's name, were well advanced by this time, and the prototype was on the road in the Spring of 1948. Much of the basic design had been thought out before the war, when an aerodynamic Volkswagen coupé had been designed for a planned road race between Rome and Berlin in 1939, though the event was cancelled and the three examples built were laid up. One survives today, owned by the Austrian Otto Mathé.

THE TYPE 356

Several views of a very desirable Porsche 356A (manufactured between 1955 and 1959) with a detachable hard-top offered by the factory to complement the Cabriolet body form. The flat-four engine looks diminutive inside the roomy engine compartment and it is the ancillaries that capture attention — the cooling fan and intake filters for the carburettors being apparent immediately. For its era, the 356A Hardtop was remarkably spacious and airy.

The original 356 used a Volkswagen 1,131 cc engine developing 38 horsepower, a VW gearbox, running gear and brakes, but it had a steel platform chassis and an aluminium spyder body, and the engine had been turned around to the mid position. Ferry Porsche, his chief engineer Karl Rabe, and designer Erwin Kommenda were responsible for the design and construction of this surprisingly lively little sports car, which weighed a mere 1,340 pounds.

In September 1948 the prototype was sold to Herr R. von Senger in Zurich, and the 7,000 Swiss francs it fetched helped to complete its successor, a 356 Coupé which also had an aluminium body. The Coupé differed in one important respect from that suggested by Professor Porsche, the engine having been turned around to overhang the rear wheels, thus making a little space behind the seats for luggage, or children's seats.

An extremely favourable report on von Senger's prototype 356 in

Green digits on black instruments were Porsche's trademark with the 356 model, but everything about the car was thoroughly functional and hard-wearing. Opening quarterlights in the front windows were an innovation for the 'A' version. The spread overleaf is of a pristine 356C model — with a non-standard rearview mirror — in Coupé form. A total of 16,674 C models were produced between 1963 and 1965 bringing total production of the 356 up to the 76,000 mark in 16 years.

the Swiss journal Automobile-Revue, created international interest, and orders began to pile up from Switzerland, Holland, Sweden, Portugal and other European countries. The problems of obtaining parts, import and export licences and so on were immense, but somehow a production line was organised and in the winter of 1948/49, the 356 Coupés were made at a rate of five per month.

Even now Dr. Ferry Porsche could not envisage a total production of more than 500 units, an underestimate of enormous proportion, perhaps born of modesty. The workforce grew to 100 and the 356 Coupé was well received when it was shown for the first time at the Geneva Salon in March 1949. By this time Dr. Porsche had come to an agreement with Volkswagen that was to prove vital in the setting up of his own manufacturing business; he was to receive a royalty of 1 DM for every Volkswagen sold. In addition, Volkswagen would sell to Porsche any line parts needed for the production of the 356, and Porsche's part of the bargain was to undertake all development work on behalf of

THE SPEEDSTER

Volkswagen. This agreement lasted some 15 years, but it needs to be stated that at no time did Volkswagen ever own, or even have shares in the Porsche company, which remains totally independent to this day.

The appeal of these small, lightweight sports cars is not difficult to pinpoint. In the austere postwar years the bigger manufacturers were turning out as many family saloons as their lines could manage, and the advent of 'popular' sports cars such as the MGA, TR2, Austin-Healey and Jaguar was yet to come. The public had been starved of exciting cars, and the Porsche 356 was the right car for the time. In today's terms the performance was not particularly outstanding; the 1.1 litre model accelerated from rest to 100 km/h (62 mph) in around 18 seconds and had a top speed of 87 miles per hour. However, it felt lively, and was extremely responsive and nimble, and still returned 35 miles to the gallon.

The Volkswagen swing axle suspension could prove difficult to master in extreme circumstances, though in such a light car it was probably easier to manage than in the heavier saloon. Without doubt,

The Speedster model was produced *specially for the California market in America, though it was sold elsewhere in the world. It was primarily an open two-seater, though rather crude weather protection was available. A total of 2,350 were made on the 356A chassis between 1955 and 1958, and are today a prime collector's model. Earlier examples had a 60 horsepower engine, later ones (as illustrated) a 75 horsepower version of the flat-four 1600 cc engine. In the photo above, the Speedster is ranged alongside the 911 Turbo, dubbed the 'Carrera Turbo' in the States.*

the particular forté of the 356 was its aerodynamic shape which, allied with light weight, enabled it to make more of its 40 (production) horsepower than most people would have thought possible. Today, more than 30 years later, the world's manufacturers are waking up to the fact that light weight and good aerodynamics are the key to energy saving, and will place increasing emphasis on the fundamental design concepts set out by Porsche as long ago as 1922, when the Sascha set a new trend.

Times change, methods don't! Today, as 20 years ago when the 356 production was in full swing, the cars are pushed from one station to another on wheeled dollies in various stages of manufacture. Modern methods are seen in the new part of the works where the 928 model is assembled, the body being lowered onto the engine/drivetrain assembly. As one nearly complete 928 is lifted away, the next chassis, complete with brakes and suspension, awaits the body coming along in the background. The pace is quite leisurely, as accuracy and quality are far more important than speed. Power units are still hand-built, and each one is dyno tested before installation.

During 1949 it became abundantly clear that Dr. Porsche's original forecast was far too pessimistic, and that a proper production line would have to be set up. It was clear, too, that the aluminium bodied cars would be difficult to produce in large numbers, even allowing for the craftsmanship and hand finishing that was to become a Porsche hallmark. Negotiations were set in motion to move back to the original Porsche works in Zuffenhausen, then occupied by the American forces, and almost adjacent to the Reutter bodywork company.

The move took place in the summer of 1950, to a factory assembly area taking up a mere 500 square metres which, before long, was sufficient to put together no fewer than 80 cars per month. Reutters were manufacturing the bodies, while the Swiss company, Beutler, was making convertible version bodies, and records show that in the first year of organised production, a total of 410 356 Coupé and Cabriolet models were sold by Porsche.

The switch to steel bodies increased the car's weight to around 1,830 pounds and to maintain, or improve, the original performance figures, an additional model was sold with a 1,300 cc engine, achieved by increasing the bore of the Volkswagen engine. Four of the original alloy bodied cars were retained by Porsche for competition work, and two of them appeared at Le Mans in 1951, the first time German cars had competed postwar on French soil. One was badly damaged during practice, but the second, in the hands of two Frenchmen, Veuillet and Mouche, won the 1,100 cc class with ease.

Since then, Le Mans has been a virtual pilgrimage for Porsche and its customers, and in the ensuing 30 years the factory has only twice failed to attend the race with factory entries, each time due to an impending change of regulations. Various international rallies were tackled by Porsche and by competition-oriented customers, resulting in a variety of successes, usually in the class. In the Rome-Liège-Rome Rally of 1951, generally reckoned to be the toughest event in the calendar, Paul von Guilleaume and Count von der Muhle finished third overall and won their class in a 356 equipped with a new engine of 1,500 cc capacity.

Gradually, the original Volkswagen parts were discarded as Porsche parts were designed to cope with the performance requirements, and put into production. The original flat-four VW engine designed by Prof. Porsche in the 1930s, and doing sterling work in the Wolfsburg saloons, was by stages bored and stroked to 1,488 cc, using new detachable cylinder barrels on the original crankcase, while power was increased to 70 horsepower, approximately double the original output.

A new four-speed gearbox with Porsche patented synchromesh was put into production, and this patent itself was to bring in handsome royalties as many leading manufacturers adopted it. Like the Volkswagen, the 356 and subsequent Porsche designs also incorporated torsion bar suspension, which was another of the Professor's patents. The standard Volkswagen brakes, adequate for the original cars, were replaced by much larger drums to Porsche's design, with alloy

CRAFTSMAN BUILT

construction to save weight and dissipate the heat better. Gradually the 356 became a 'real Porsche', the product of Zuffenhausen.

Professor Ferdinand Porsche, one of the world's greatest automotive pioneers, died in January 1952 at the age of 76. His health had never recovered from postwar internment and he was laid to rest at Zell am See, the family home in Austria. Porsche followers from all over the world attended a memorial service at which the German Minister of Transport paid tribute to the great man, saying: "Ferdinand Porsche was the last of the great designers whose name was famous all over the world. He belonged to the likes of Daimler, Benz, Bugatti and Lancia whose names denote the make of a motor car."

Having singled out the tough Rome-Liège-Rome Rally for mention in the previous year, we must not fail to mention the 1952 event, which saw Porsches taking first, third and fourth places in the overall results, beating a host of works teams which invariably had larger and more powerful engines. The hillclimbing ability and general agility of these 70 horsepower, 1,500 cc engined alloy coupés enabled them to run rings round cars which were potentially much faster on a straight road.

By this time the 356 was also available in Britain, though initially only to Americans and diplomats, and it was not until 1953, when A.F.N. Limited took on the concession, that the Porsche became generally available. The Isleworth company, founded by Archie Frazer

It was his son, Ferry, who laid the foundations for the Porsche company as a manufacturer of world renown, who negotiated the astute and probably all-important contract with Volkswagen which gave Porsche a ready-made service network, and who capitalised on the firm's extraordinary talents for design on a consultancy basis. Today this is one of the most profitable areas of the company's operation, as will be shown in a later chapter.

By 1952 the fortunes of the company had really taken off, and export sales alone would have been enough to keep the production line at full swing. At the suggestion of the American importer, a Speedster version of the 356 was introduced, this being an open car with a vestigial hood arrangement particularly suited to the Californian climate. More and more cars were being sold with the 1,300 cc and 1,500 cc engines, developing 44 and 55 bhp respectively, with the addition of a 1300S engine rated at 60 bhp and a 1500S rated at 70 bhp.

Engine blocks are mounted on swivelling jigs, whether they be 911 motors (above) or 928 V8s (right), enabling the assemblers to work around them without *any discomfort. The sound of air-driven wrenches is characteristic of this area of the Zuffenhausen works.*

Nash in the 1920s, had long been the birthplace of the Frazer-Nash sports car which had done so well in all manner of rallies, races and sporting trials. A.F.N. Limited had also imported BMWs in the prewar years, but by 1953 the production of Frazer-Nash cars was nearing an end and the Aldington family were looking for a new string to their bow. The Porsche marque provided that string, and the success of the marriage was such that before long A.F.N Limited was solely occupied with importing and selling Porsches. In the mid-1960s a separate company, Porsche Cars Great Britain Limited, was founded to act as the concessionnaire, leaving A.F.N. free to concentrate on London sales while a countrywide dealer network was established.

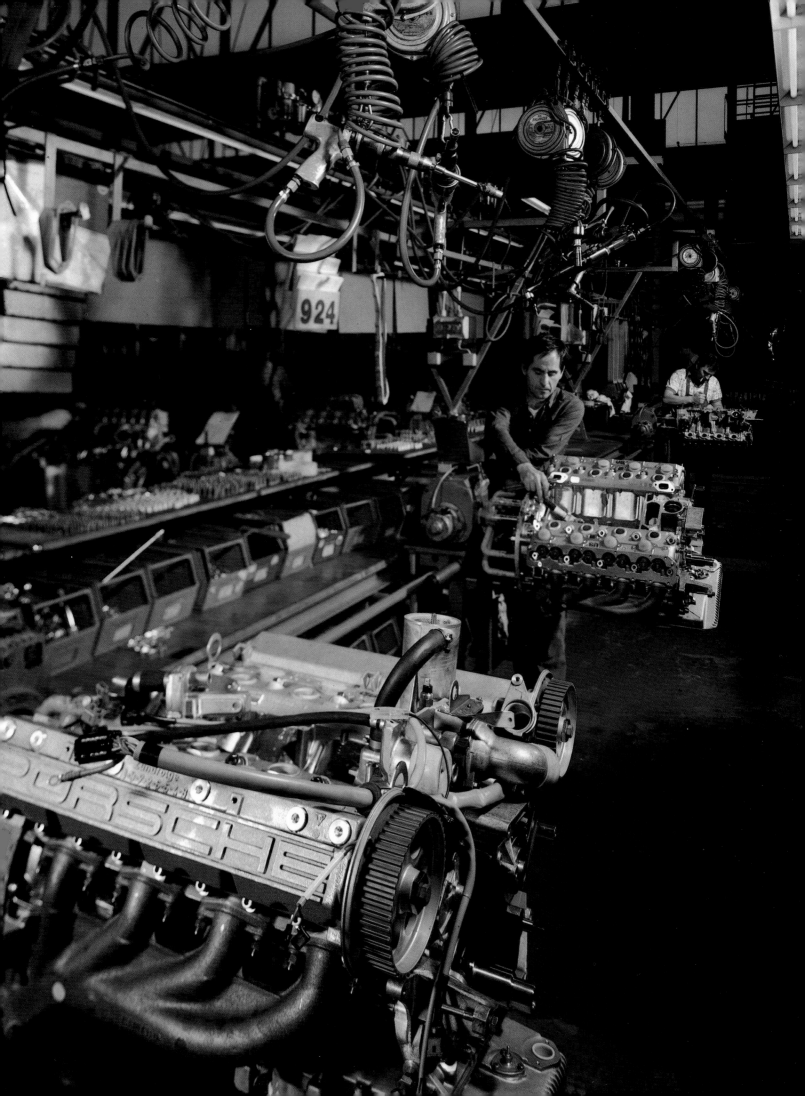

Two more 356s (these pages) prepared to Concours standards, as only the Americans know how! The imitation knock-on hubs on the 356A Coupé might not be to everyone's taste, but the B hardtop *is a real beauty. The extremely high standard of preparation attained by the enthusiast is well illustrated by the magnificent vehicles shown overleaf.*

Throughout the 1950s the Porsche works grew apace, as the company's records show. In 1950, when Porsche moved to Zuffenhausen, a total of 108 workers produced 298 cars and the turnover was 4.4 million Deutschemarks. By 1959 the firm employed 1,100 people, produced 7,600 cars in the year and had a turnover of 90 million Deutschemarks—and to this total should be added the Porsche tractor production in Friedrichshafen, which peaked in 1958 at 17,000 units. In 1962, the tractor business was sold, enabling Porsche to concentrate on car production.

As to the development of the cars, the Volkswagen crankcase was superseded in 1954 by a stronger Porsche design, better able to cope with the power, so that little remained of the VW origins. Taking matters a stage further, a special Carrera engine was designed by Dr. Ernst Fuhrmann, who was later to leave the company for a spell and return as managing director between 1972 and 1980. This four-cam 1,500 cc unit developed 95 horespower and took the maximum speed up to 125 mph, and in 1962 the capacity was taken up to a full 2-litres and 130 horsepower, making the Carrera 2 the fastest production Porsche ever made.

Porsche standardised on a 1,582 cc engine developing 60 or 75 horsepower from 1957, with a 90 bhp 'Super' version added in 1960.

Chassis development never ceased, with a revised 356A version being announced in 1955, a 356B version in 1959 and the final 356C version in 1962. Each revision made the cars more comfortable and more refined. Exports accounted for around 70 per cent of production, with 50 per cent going to the States and the remainder being distributed throughout Europe, Australia and South Africa.

On the competitions side, the type 550 model took over the 356's pioneering work in 1953 powered by the first versions of Dr. Fuhrmann's four-cam engine. Throughout the 1950s the 550 and its successor, the 718, became near-certain class winners in all manner of races, hillclimbs, rallies and other speed events. Always a favourite event for Porsche was the Targa Florio, a magnificent race on closed public roads in Sicily, which resulted in outright wins in 1956 and again in 1959. Gradually the factory became more ambitious, and after developing a successful Formula 2 car in the late 1950s, went on to design a flat-eight engined Formula 1 car which American Dan Gurney took to victory in the French Grand Prix of 1962.

When the 356 model was finally discontinued in 1965, a total of more than 76,000 had been manufactured, exceeding Dr. Porsche's estimate by a very wide margin. The Porsche marque was now pre-eminent among the world's sports car manufacturers.

VW-PORSCHE 914

Planning a new model is vital for any car manufacturer, for if the ingredients aren't right and the newcomer doesn't have sales appeal it can have a nasty, adverse effect on the balance sheets. For Porsche, though, the replacement of the 356 would be absolutely vital, for there were no other models to fall back on. The new car would have to replace the 356 in the hearts, minds and pockets of many thousand customers ...except that these were no ordinary customers, but true aficionados. If it failed, the company would not survive.

The replacement was entrusted to Ferdinand Porsche III, nick-named 'Butzi', as head of styling and his cousin Ferdinand Piëch, who headed the engine development team. There was a measure of opinion that the 901 (as the new car was designated) should be a full four seater, but preliminary designs were rejected by Ferry Porsche on the grounds that his company made *sports* cars, and had no wish to compete with Mercedes, on the other side of Stuttgart.

The design brief was for a car which would have more interior space than the 356, more comfort, more luggage capacity and higher performance. From the start it was to have a two-litre six cylinder engine, still air cooled and rear mounted. Longitudinal torsion bar suspension at the front made more space for the luggage, fuel tank and spare wheel, while the rear suspension employed transverse torsion bars. Semi trailing arm suspension location and articulated driveshafts would finally overcome the dreaded swing axle tendencies of the 356, and disc brakes all round would ensure adequate stopping power.

Four prototypes were made, and one, the 821, was similar to the final design in most respects except that it had a wet sump engine— the

A hybrid, maybe, but a production run of 125,000 in five years spells success. The VW-Porsche 914 (these pages) was produced by a company set up jointly by Volkswagen and Porsche, the 914/4 powered by Volkswagen's four cylinder engines and the 914/6 by Porsche's 2-litre six. The cars were the best-handling models produced to date by either company for series production.

911 has dry sump lubrication, which is a more expensive but technically superior method of force-feeding the bearings. In final production form the 911's engine developed 130 horsepower, sufficient to give the car a top speed of 131 mph and acceleration from rest to 100 km/h (62 mph) in 8.5 seconds.

The Porsche 901 made its debut at the Frankfurt Motor Show in September 1963, following up with appearances at the Paris and

THE BIRTH OF THE 911

London Shows. It was not in fact scheduled for production until autumn 1964, but there was tremendous interest in the car right from the start. The 901 retained a family likeness to the 356 but was less bulbous (being 2½ inches narrower, yet more spacious inside), had a five inch longer wheelbase and was six inches longer overall. The glass area was increased by a full 50 per cent, improving all-round visibility and making the car feel more airy for the occupants.

A four-cylinder 1,600 cc version was also destined for production, using a 90 horsepower edition of the 356's ubiquitous pushrod power unit. Before production commenced the type number of the 901 had to be changed to 911, after Peugeot objected to the designation; the French firm had apparently registered three-figure numbers with a zero in the middle for its saloons. The four-cylinder car was designated the 912.

To prepare for the new car, Porsche took over the neighbouring Reutter bodywork plant and updated their own works, though not compromising in the slightest on the craftsmanship that goes into each car. Even today, as 4,000 workers produce up to 16,000 cars anually at Zuffenhausen, visitors are struck by the care that is taken by the men and women at every stage of assembly, contrasting strongly with the streamlined, mechanised processes of the mass producers.

The Porsche newcomer was greeted enthusiastically by customers and Press alike. American journalist Jerry Sloniger, writing the first English language test report, commented that the standard model 911 compared very favourably with the 356 Carrera 2 version on price and performance, but that the new engine and five-speed gearbox were notably smoother. Disc brakes on all four wheels (incorporating Porsche's unique parking brake drums in the centres of the rear discs), were well up to the 911's performance, and if there was a criticism, it was that too much road shake was transmitted through the new rack and pinion steering system to the large, wood rimmed steering wheel.

Speeds in the gears were: 35 mph in first, 65 mph in second, 95 mph in third, 120 mph in fourth and 131 mph in overdrive fifth, but Sloniger's rest-to-60 mph acceleration time was a slightly disappointing 8.7 seconds. The new suspension system passed its test with flying colours, and the airy interior was much praised, not least because it made the car easier to place when driving or parking.

Sloniger concluded: "The 356 is still going strong after 15 years and I would hazard a guess that the 911 will be at least as long-lived, if not more so. It suits the age—better than those fours do now".

Those early examples weren't by any means perfect. Six single-

choke Solex carburetters had replaced the three twin-choke carbs on the 901, and there was an appreciable flat-spot when the throttle was snapped open. Of more concern was the sharp understeering characteristic, perhaps more than the designers intended to achieve in their efforts to mask the natural oversteering tendency of a car with its engine overslung at the back. Weights concealed in the front bumpers could be used to reduce the problem, if the customer so desired!

The Porsche 911 made an auspicious competitions debut in the Monte Carlo Rally run in January 1965, just four months after production had started. Porsche engineers Herbert Linge and Peter Falk drove the car in blizzard conditions to fifth place overall, and a 2-litre class win, which was a marvellous boost for the 911 at just the right time. Inevitably, among the hardcore of 356 owners there was a suspicious feeling that the 911 wasn't "a proper Porsche," but good competitions results completely overcame this prejudice. And as time would prove, the 911 was to become by far the most prolific winner ever made by Porsche, its successes probably exceeding the total number of wins achieved by the company's many racing car designs.

In the first full year of production, Porsche's Zuffenhausen factory was working at capacity, turning out 6,440 912s, 4,865 911s and the last

Shown on these pages in Coupé and Targa forms, the 911 offers a choice of open or closed sportscar motoring. The Carrera, (above) is the most powerful normally aspirated 911 built for general sale, rated at 210 horsepower. (Overleaf): A silver 911 Coupé and a chocolate brown Targa and (inset) the Porsche 928 model, a green 911 Targa to European specifications, profile of the 928, 911 Turbo 303, and the latest 911 Coupé.

EVOLUTION

This 911T was one of three 911 versions built in the late 1960s, T denoting 'Touring' trim. The 911S was the most powerful, the 911E was the standard fuel injected model. The 911T illustrated, which was incidentally the last normally aspirated series production Porsche (rather than having Bosch fuel injection), was the basis on which Porsche tackled a number of sporting events with a great deal of success, notably three wins in the Monte Carlo Rally in 1968-69-70. The five-spoke polished forged alloy wheels fitted to this car are virtually a Porsche trademark.

1,688 356s, which took total production beyond the 76,000 mark.

The 912 model is interesting, in that although it was never particularly popular with Porsche enthusiasts, a total of just over 30,000 examples were built in four years. It sold at a price of DM 16,250, a little more than the 356 that it superseded, but some DM 7,000 less than the new 911. For that, it offered the smart new bodyshape, the latest chassis developments, but the old engine and a four-speed gearbox (the five-speed box cost an extra DM 340). The performance wasn't exactly exhilarating, with a 0-60 mph acceleration time of 12 seconds and a top speed of 115 mph, but there was a steady market for the model …not everyone who really wanted a Porsche could afford the full price of the 911.

One thing that was missing from the range was a convertible, and this was rectified early in 1966 with the Targa version of the 911 and 912. "Targa" is an abbreviation of Targa Florio, the Sicilian road race which

The 911 Turbo was first produced with a 3-litre engine, turning out 240 horsepower, for the American market, and 260 horsepower for the rest of the world. Turbocharging, adopted by Porsche to dominate the Can-Am racing series in 1972 and 1973, is exhaust driven supercharging and allows higher engine outputs to be achieved in exhilarating fashion without putting undue strain on the engine. Porsche and Pirelli jointly developed the P7 tyre especially for this model, offering a superb combination of grip and driveability.

THE TURBO

A production prototype of the 911 Turbo (facing page) had the vented grille below the rear number plate, but this didn't appear in production despite the very high temperatures realised in this area by the turbocharger, which spins at up to 90,000 rpm! The current 3.3 litre version of the 911 Turbo, (this page) may be identified by the different shape of the rear aerodynamic wing which further reduces 'lift' at high speed. The 3.3, rated at 300 horsepower, is one of the world's fastest production cars with a top speed of 160 mph, and acceleration from rest to 100 mph in 12.6 seconds. The 3.3, which went into production in 1978, features cross-drilled brake discs which, internally ventilated as well, are derived from the type 917 racing car. Also shown is the latest model 911 from which the Turbo is developed.

Porsche had already succeeded in winning four times, (just as the appellation Carrera for a top-performance Porsche was derived from the Carrera Panamericana Mexico road race, in which Porsche had taken a famous class victory some years before). The Targa top consisted of a steel roll-over hoop which was nicely styled for the body shape, a fixed or detachable rear window, and a folding removable soft-top, the combination of which allowed snug winter motoring or a draught-free mode of summer travel.

Later in 1966 came another development eagerly awaited by Porsche fans, the 911S model. Various engine modifications raised the power output to 160 horsepower, thicker ventilated disc brakes were

rolled off the lines, a Targa 911 model destined for service with the German police autobahn patrols. By this time the 911 and 912 models were being made at a rate of 13,000 to 14,000 a year, and Porsche employed nearly 4,000 people.

In the 18 years since the prototype 356 had first appeared, Porsche had grown into a serious manufacturer of high repute, with a solid base and a good worldwide distribution and service network. Porsche had not, and will never, become a mass manufacturer; to compete even against BMW would involve a massive injection of capital into production, much higher risks, and eventually the loss of the mystique which surrounds a quality product. Rather, Porsche remains the largest

fitted, and wider wheels with improved tyre equipment called for flared wheel arches.

The 911S offered an outstanding road car, with a 60 mph acceleration time of around 7.4 seconds and a top speed of 140 mph; today such a car is a real collector's item. The five-spoke polished alloy wheels, incidentally, virtually became a Porsche trademark in the years to come.

Just before Christmas in 1966 the 100,000th production Porsche

of the world's specialist car manufacturers, operating with the economies of scale which exceed those of Ferrari, Maserati or Aston-Martin, for instance.

The Monte Carlo Rally is surely the most glamorous of the world's rally events, and in 1968 the British crew, Vic Elford and David Stone, won the event outright in a works Porsche 911T—by this time there were several distinct versions of the 911, the T (for Touring) version having a less luxurious, therefore lighter interior trim but still having the most powerful engine available for competitions. Porsche had won the Spa 24-hour Touring Car race two years running with the 911T homologated as a saloon car, and to the opposition it looked as though the Zuffenhausen company had a car capable of winning almost every category in racing or rallying. The 1968 Monte Carlo Rally win was followed a year later with another victory, this time by the Swedish driver Bjorn Waldegaard.

Though improved year by year, the first major design change was seen in 1969, when the engine capacity was increased to 2.2 litres; achieved by increasing the six-cylinder bore from 80 to 84 mm while

the six-cylinder was rather expensive and failed to match the performance and versatility of the larger-engined 911 range.

A main feature of the 914 was that the engine was mounted ahead of the rear wheels in racing car fashion—just as Ferry Porsche had designed the prototype 356. It meant that the car was an uncompromising two-seater, but it also resulted in the 914 having the best handling characteristics of any Porsche designed up to that time. Today, a late, 2 litre 914/4 fuel injected model, or better still a six-cylinder 914/6, would command a high value.

By 1969 the Porsche factory employed 3,713 people producing 15,275 cars, which was just about full capacity. Sixty per cent were

1

leaving the stroke at 66 mm. Now the Touring version developed 125 horsepower, the E version (with fuel injection): 155 horsepower, and the S version: 180 horsepower. A year earlier, the wheelbase had been extended by 57 mm, which had the effect of improving the weight distribution and handling characteristics, and with ventilated disc brakes being available on all models the whole Porsche range could now appeal to keen drivers, whilst offering adequate comfort and sophistication for those who wished to use their pride and joy for business and family purposes.

It was in 1969 that Porsche and Volkswagen set up a separate joint-stock company based in Ludwigsburg, to produce the Volkswagen-Porsche 914 sports car. The square looking body shape, designed and developed by Porsche, housed either a four-cylinder Volkswagen engine (originally of 1.6 litres but later, by stages, increased to 1.7, 1.8, and 2-litres with fuel injection), or a 2-litre Porsche 6-cylinder engine. Around 125,000 VW-Porsches were produced in five years, so by no stretch of the imagination could the model be termed anything other than a success…yet the models never quite captured the minds of Porsche loyalists. The VW powered version, which effectively succeeded the 912 model, was considered a little too noisy and slow, while

Cross sections of the Porsche 928 (1), 924 (2) and 911 (3) show some family traits. The 911, which first appeared in public in 1963, has its air-cooled engine overslung at the rear and full torsion bar suspension, thus revealing its ancestry back to Professor Porsche and the 356 model.

The 924, which made its debut in 1975, and the 928 which was announced in 1978, both have engines at the front and transmissions at the rear in transaxle form to achieve equal weight distributions at the front and back, thus giving them excellent roadholding.

exported to America (California alone taking half the total) and it was a sign of the times that many were equipped with Sportomatic transmission. This was a semi-automatic box with four forward gears, but instead of a clutch pedal, the mechanism relied on a magnetic particle operated clutch with a solenoid in the gear lever knob. A torque converter was installed and there was a slight loss of efficiency, but the 2.2 litre engine was sufficiently powerful to allow more than adequate performance. If nothing else, the system cured people of driving around with a hand on the gear lever!

In 1970 Porsche produced 16,761 cars and the total company turnover rose to DM 420 million. A further mechanical improvement for the 1972 model year (the company's model years run from August to August), was to increase the engine capacity again to 2.4 litres, this time

by fitting a new crankshaft and connecting rods to increase the stroke to 70.4 millimetres. Significantly, the compression ratios were reduced so that all engines, even the 190 bhp 'S' version, could run on commercial grade fuel.

Porsche suffered its first serious setback in 1971, when the American market slumped badly, partly on account of the worsening dollar/Deutschemark exchange rate, and production dropped sharply to 11,715 cars, while turnover fell by 25 per cent. A three-week strike, the first in Porsche's history, added to the trouble, and the workforce was put onto a four day week. It was at this time that the management itself was going through a crisis period, and Dr. Porsche's solution was to ask members of his, and the Piëch families, to look elsewhere for employment. His eldest son 'Butzi' returned to Austria to set up a now renowned styling studio, while Ferdinand Piëch quit the research and development centre to become chief of development at Audi (the Quattro is one of his better known achievements there).

THE CARRERA

Dr. Ernst Fuhrmann returned to the company as chairman of the executive board, and Ing. Helmuth Bott was promoted to the directorship of the Weissach research and development centre with responsibility for Porsche's model development, racing activities, and for outside contracts.

The shareholding of the company was split into 10 equal parts among members of the two families, Dr. Porsche and his four sons having half the shares, his sister Frau Louise Piëch, her three sons and one daughter having the remainder. Dr. Porsche, however, heads the supervisory board, which is responsible for the longterm planning and development of the firm, and in that sense still controls the company.

Fortunes of the company were on the upturn in 1972 as production rose to 14,500 cars, and the celebration took the form of the announcement of what remains a classic in the 911 series; the 2.7 litre Carrera RS model. We have explained that the Carrera name is sometimes given to the most powerful car in the range, but more than that, it denotes that the model is intended for further development for competitions. Just over 1,000 Carreras were made in the initial batch, all with mechanically fuel injected engines developing 210 horsepower, lightened bodywork and simplified (almost Spartan) interior trim. These cars, which could accelerate from rest to 60 mph in six seconds 1

Several generations of Porsche are shown in these pictures, dating from the 356 prototype leading the convoy (3) to the latest 911 SC model (1 and 2). Impact absorbing bumpers have been available for the 911s since 1973 — and standard for the British market — along with electrically operated sunroofs and other luxury items.

3

and reach close on 150 miles per hour, vied with the Jaguar E-type for performance, though having little more than half the Jaguar's engine capacity. In racing trim they became virtually certain Grand Touring class winners on the world's racing circuits for the next three years and captured numerous championships.

Having introduced turbocharging to the Can-Am (Canadian-American Racing Championship) series in 1972/73, Porsche decided to develop this promising method of obtaining more engine power. In 1974 the factory racing team extensively campaigned a turbocharged 911 Carrera RSR in the World Championship for Makes, the best result being second place overall at Le Mans. This was the prelude to one of Porsche's most famous road cars, the 911 Turbo, which made its world debut at the Paris motor show in October 1974.

The production version of the 911 Turbo had a full 3-litre version of the air-cooled flat-six engine, developed in fact from the final version of the Carrera RS. But with turbocharging applied, the Turbo model developed no less than 260 horsepower and gave the proud owner simply electrifying road performance: acceleration to 60 mph in under six seconds, and a top speed of 155 miles per hour, placing this model right into the Supercar class, competing against the best that Ferrari, Lamborghini, Maserati and Aston-Martin could offer. The 911 Turbo

Even the police use Porsches, notably in Germany and in Holland (previous page), these being Targa models with the one-time option of fold-down rear windows.

One Californian couldn't make up his mind whether he preferred black or Minerva blue...so he had both! These 3.3 litre Turbos have non-standard BBS wheels and the blue car on this page has a smart looking customised interior. Both cars can reach the Californian 55 mph speed limit in around five seconds flat, but it's the way you do it that really counts! Imports of the Turbo model to America virtually ceased in 1980 due to new emission rules coming into force, but the model remains much sought after. With air conditioning the Turbo has every comfort.

was originally intended for limited production for homologation purposes, which meant that with a production of 500 examples in twelve months, Porsche could claim this to be a production car and could race developments of it in World Championship class racing from 1976 onwards. As history shows, demand for this wonderful motor car exceeded all expectations and Porsche made over 8,000 examples in the next seven production years.

Step-by-step evolution in Porsche's range saw the 911 model made up to 2.7 litres in 1973 (the 'basic' model produced 150 bhp, the 'S' version 175 bhp, and the production Carrera version 210 bhp), while in 1975 the mechanically injected Carrera RS was discontinued and replaced by the more luxurious Carrera 3 model, with a 200 bhp normally aspirated version of the Turbo's 3-litre engine.

Then, in 1977 came a further development, which brings us virtually up to date. The Turbo model was increased in capacity to 3.3 litres and the power was augmented to 300 horsepower with the help of an air-to-air intercooler, which reduces the temperature of the compressed air from the turbocharger and thus improves combustion efficiency. The Carrera 3 model was dropped, and the standard 911 SC model was taken up to 3-litres and 180 horsepower.

Further development stopped for a while as the larger engined V8 powered 928 model was introduced, but went ahead again in 1981 when an American, Peter Schutz, replaced Prof. Dr. Fuhrmann as chairman of the executive board. With production of the 911 and Turbo assured for some years to come, two further developments of the 911 were seen at the Frankfurt Show in 1981. One was fully convertible (cabriolet) bodywork based on the 911 Targa model, the other a four-wheel drive system for the Turbo model.

Two important milestones were reached in September 1981, when the "911 Studie" appeared at the Frankfurt Show, as the 200,000th 911 model built, and later in the month the 300,000th Porsche rolled off the Zuffenhausen line. This total, incidentally, excludes the 100,000-plus 924 models that have been made in Neckarsulm, and puts the seal on the foundation and expansion of a family dynasty.

THE NEW GENERATION

If the commercial success of the 356 had taken Dr. Porsche by surprise, he knew that its replacement by the 911 was something of a gamble which must succeed. Now firmly established as a major manufacturer of sports cars with worldwide markets, the Porsche company had to diversify in the 1970s so that the risk factors, always present, could be reduced. The 911 model was moving steadily upmarket to the 3-litre class, so what was needed was a new 2-litre model with popular appeal, to bring new customers into the fold… and then a bigger and more powerful car to retain these customers' loyalty when they wanted something more than the 911 could offer.

The VW-Porsche company was quietly buried in 1974, a hard year for all motor manufacturers. Porsche had already lost interest, as the six-cylinder model was not sufficiently popular, while Volkswagen was undergoing a cashflow crisis, as the Golf and Polo models came on stream to replace the ageing Beetle. In fact, Porsche had already

The 924 model (right) and the 924 Turbo derivative broke entirely new ground for Porsche, giving the German company a far greater market than it had enjoyed before. The two-litre four cylinder engine develops 125 bhp for the 924, and 177 bhp with the turbocharger for the Turbo model. Then came the 944, production commencing in 1982, and the new Porsche designed all-aluminium engine which sets new standards for power and economy. The 2½-litre 944 has twin counterbalance shafts which make the four-cylinder engine every bit as smooth as a good 'six'.*

The chassis of the 944 is based on that of the 924 Carrera GT, using the same front engine/rear transaxle principle for good weight distribution. The big four-cylinder engine fits snugly into the front compartment, mounted on hydraulic dampers to reduce the already low noise level. The V8 engine of the 928, (above)

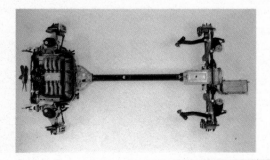

all aluminium with linerless construction, hydraulic tappets, and 300 horsepower in its more powerful 'S' version. The transaxle layout is clearly shown in the illustration, a 25mm shaft taking the power from the twin-plate clutch (or torque converter) to the manual or automatic gearbox at the rear.

designed and built prototypes of a 2-litre sports car for Volkswagen, using VW-Audi based components for the engine, gearbox and brakes, and felt sufficiently committed to this project to buy out Volkswagen's investment. The entire design was Porche's, after all, and late in 1975 the newcomer was added to the Porsche range as the 924 model.

By normal standards, the 924 is conventional in most respects, but to Porsche it was rather radical. Seeing that the 914 mid-engined concept had certain advantages (mostly in roadholding) and definite disadvantages (interior capacity), Porsche had undertaken a number of experiments and come up with the best solution, which involved a 'transaxle' system—that is, placing the gearbox at the rear of the car, between the driven wheels. By moving this mass to the rear, and thereby moving the engine back about 12 inches in the chassis, it was possible to achieve virtually equal weight distribution, with 51 per cent on the front wheels, 49 per cent on the rear. That the 924 had excellent handling was immediately clear; others, notably Alfa Romeo, had experimented with transaxle layouts, but the gearchange wasn't always as good as it should have been. With a true sports car, rather than a sporting saloon, Porsche seemed to have broken new ground.

The front engine is water cooled (Volkswagen having broken

One enterprising Stateside Porsche dealer shows how to customise a 924 Turbo to good effect. On the facing page, the Turbo is fitted with BBS wheels, flared wheel arches also featuring warm air extractors, and a new bib spoiler which contrasts with the standard model on this page. In America Porsches and Audis are marketed by the same company, but that's as far as the connection goes, Porsche being an independent company with ten private shareholders, who are all members of the Porsche and related Piëch families. The 924 Turbo model offers an exciting blend of performance and 2-litre fuel economy, ever more important these days.

down the prejudices with the Beetle replacement!), and develops 125 horsepower, drive being taken through the clutch—adjacent to the flywheel —to the rear transaxle by means of a small diameter torque tube. MacPherson strut front suspension contrasts with Porsche's traditional torsion bar rear suspension, and similarly, modern disc brakes at the front are used in conjunction with drums at the rear. Another distinct advantage of the transaxle, and having the engine further back in the chassis than is normal, is the possibility of a very clean shape for the car, as well as a low drag coefficient, quoted at 0.36.

The 924 model may not have delighted the 911 devotees, but it was widely accepted in the world markets as a quick, reliable and very economical Porsche, available with four (later five) speed manual transmission or a fully automatic box. That 100,000 were made in five years speaks for the acceptability of this two-plus-two seater model which, like everything else in the range, carries a seven-year anti corrosion warranty.

1

2

3

following January. This had an unusually large engine for a four-cylinder, at 2.5 litres, but was constructed in aluminium and featured twin, contra-rotating counterbalance shafts which smooth out the inherent imbalance. With advanced techniques in combustion, injection and ignition the 944, which has the Carrera's ventilated disc brakes and other chassis developments, produces 163 horsepower and offers very high performance combined with excellent torque and economy ratings.

While the 924 was under development, initially as an outside contract, Porsche's Weissach team was concentrating on a totally new luxury car, which made its debut at the Geneva Show in 1978. The 928, although bearing a family likeness to the 924 and having the same front engine, rear transaxle layout, was a totally new car throughout—longer, wider, more roomy than the 924 and the 911, and powered by a lightweight 240 horsepower V8 engine of 4,474 cc. It offered five-speed manual or three-speed automatic transmissions and a high level of performance and comfort. The 928's success was guaranteed when it

A good cross-section of Porsche's offerings today.
Facing page, (1) the limited production Carrera GT with a body shape that set the style for the 944. (2), The 928S and (3), the 924. On this page, a front view of the 924 (4) which is the Press demonstrator operated by Porsche Cars Great Britain Ltd. The 928 and 928S (5) cater for Porsche's wealthier clientèle, while the 911 Targa (6) remains as popular as ever. (7), The first 944 with right-hand drive. Overleaf, American specification 911 Targa and 924 Turbo featuring the heavy but practical bumper protection.

A turbocharged version was announced in 1978 with the same 2-litre engine base uprated to 170 horsepower, and later to 177 horsepower. With ventilated disc brakes and a stronger transmission, the 924 Turbo was altogether more acceptable to the Porsche traditionalists, for it had abundant power without sacrificing economy. In 1980 the ultimate 924 appeared as a limited edition, as 400 of the 924 Carrera GT cars were made. The turbocharged engine was fitted with an intercooler and uprated to 210 horsepower, as the homologated basis for a competition model, which ran successfully at Le Mans in 1980 and in 1981.

Customers awaiting a true, Porsche-engined 924, were rewarded when the 944 model was announced in 1981, for production starting the

was awarded the "Car of the Year 1978" accolade by an international jury of motoring writers.

In 1980 an even quicker 928S model was added to the range, the alloy V8 engine being enlarged to 4.7 litres and no less than 300 horsepower. With improved braking and a higher trim level, this had more appeal, perhaps, to those who enjoyed 911 performance to the full, and within a year production of the 'S' version was higher than that of the 4.5 litre version.

In the space of seven years Porsche had progressed from offering a single model (911) in three versions, to a full range of cars for a very wide selection of customers. The full range was: the 924, the 924 Turbo, the 944, 911 SC, 911 Turbo, 928 and 928S.

THE RACING LINE

The two great dynasties in postwar motor racing are those of Porsche and Ferrari. Both companies have a long and highly successful record in endurance racing, but whereas Ferrari has always put Grand Prix events at the forefront of his programme, Porsche remained faithful to the concept of racing production, or production based cars, in long distance épreuves. For a brief period in the late fifties and early sixties, Porsche did enter the worlds of Formula 2 and Formula 1 racing, with success, but Dr. Porsche was never convinced that the astronomic costs involved were justified by the results. If you look at the production records and financial results of the two companies, you might decide that Porsche's approach was the right one.

Early successes in racing and rallying were achieved by customers using the aluminium bodied 356 coupés, which were usually good for a win in the 1,100 cc class. Porsche's first foray into motor racing as a "factory" was in 1951, when Charles Faroux, organiser of the Le Mans 24-Hour event, persuaded Dr. Porsche to put in an official entry. This was to be the first appearance by a German racing team on French soil since the war, and Porsche was a little apprehensive about this, but the event passed off without mishap. The French Porsche importer, Auguste Veuillet, and his co-driver Mouche, had a trouble-free run to a class win, and the Porsche factory has had an almost unbroken record of participation at Le Mans in the ensuing 30 years.

Encouraged by innumerable successes in long distance racing, Porsche made a brief sortie into single-seaters (1 and 3) in the period 1958 to 1962. The Formula 2 type 718/2 (2) was built in 1960, using a 1½-litre four cylinder engine in common with the type 356B Carrera Abarth and the type 718/RS 60 competition cars in the same picture. In 1962 came the type 804 Formula 1 car using a new flat eight cylinder engine, also of 1½-litres to comply with the current regulations. Dan Gurney, the American driver, scored Porsche's only Grand Prix victory at Rouen in France that year.

On the facing page, a miscellany of Porsche's most successful endurance racing cars of the 1960s and 1970s. (1), The spaceframe 906 model designed primarily for private owners, though also used effectively by the factory on occasions. It was followed by the 908 model in Coupé or Spyder forms (2 and 4), while (3) shows the popular 904 model produced in 1964. (5) shows a private development, the 908 with a 2.1-litre turbocharged engine seen here driven by the late Herbert Mueller.

1

2

3

4

5

CUSTOMER RACERS

There was one outstanding success where perhaps Porsche least expected it, as private owners took five of the top ten places in the 1952 Liège-Rome-Liège rally. The German crew, Polensky and Schluter, won the arduous rally using the newly developed 1,500 cc engine; Porsches also finished third, fourth, ninth and tenth overall. These aluminium bodied cars had a whole string of successes in the early 1950s, but Porsche soon felt that a more potent car would be needed by the works team and its customers, and in 1953 a strange-looking car nicknamed "the hunchback" appeared. Officially, this was known as the type 550 Porsche Spyder, a purpose built open two-seater for competitions. It had a new tubular frame chassis and was powered by a 1,500 cc four-camshaft engine designed by Dr. Fuhrmann, one of the company's brightest young engineers. The engine developed 110 horsepower initially, and the 550 made a brief and secret appearance during practice for the sports car race that supported the German Grand Prix. It wasn't particularly fast to begin with, and further development was needed for

the 1954 season. Despite continuing development problems the 550 won its class in the classic Mille Miglia race (finishing sixth overall), and again at Le Mans, although two of the three works cars retired with holed pistons.

From that point on, the 550 became the most powerful entry in the 1,500 cc class in all manner of events, and completely eclipsed the 356 production model. More than 100 replicas were made and sold, mostly in America, so that the 550 became virtually a production model in its own right. Inevitably, other manufacturers eventually caught up, and Porsche produced an 'RS' version of the type 550 with 130 horsepower, a lighter but strengthened chassis, and a new five-speed gearbox. This ensured Porsche's continued supremacy in the class, and enabled the company to realise one of its top ambitions: to win the Targa Florio race outright. Italian driver Umberto Maglioli put in a sterling single-handed drive in this gruelling Sicilian event in 1956, a feat which hasn't been repeated.

The following year, Porsche's interest in single-seater racing was kindled, as the 1½ litre Formula 2 regulations coincided with the RS design. Edgar Barth drove the RS in the Eifel Formula 2 race, and to everyone's astonishment won quite easily against the rear-engined, purpose built single-seaters, probably assisted by the sportscar body-work which was more aerodynamically efficient. For 1958, therefore,

Two of Porsche's best loved competition cars for sale were the 904 model produced in 1964, and the Carrera 6 which came out two years later. The 904, usually powered by a four-cylinder engine, had a monocoque construction which made it particularly durable — one even finished second in the 1965 Monte Carlo Rally.

The Carrera 6 usually had a six-cylinder engine though the factory prototypes had eight cylinder units installed. The 904, and then the 906, won the 2-litre division in countless events during the 1960s the whole world over; the 904 was powered by the 356's four cylinder unit, the 906 by the 911's six cylinder unit.

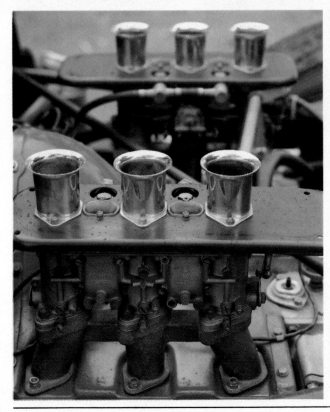

WORLD CHAMPIONS

Porsche made a central-seater version of the RS, officially named the type 718 RSK, with its engine now tuned up to around 155 horsepower. Jean Behra, the leading French driver, easily won the Formula 2 race at Rheims, but this was the only notable success of the season.

There were more successes in 1959 and in 1960, leading Porsche directly into Formula 1. As the regulations changed in 1961, bringing the engine capacity down to 1½ litres, Porsche decided to tackle the heights of Grand Prix racing, initially with the Carrera engine, and in 1962 with a completely new flat-eight cylinder unit, still air cooled, in a new chassis. The American driver, Dan Gurney, recorded the Porsche team's single success in the French Grand Prix of 1962, held at Rheims. The Formula 1 Porsche remained competitive throughout the year, but Porsche realised with 'only' 180 horsepower available compared with 200 bhp for their main rivals, they would be drawn into an expensive power race, and reluctantly decided not to carry on. Porsche has not built another single-seater in the past 20 years.

challenge the winning Mini-Cooper driven by Timo Makinen. In fifth place overall was the Porsche 911, making its debut in the hands of Porsche technicians Herbert Linge and Peter Falk.

When, in 1966, Ferdinand Piëch was appointed head of Porsche's research and development, the company embarked on a costly but supremely effective programme of racing car development. Formula 1 may have been ruled out on the grounds of cost, but Porsche as a company spent as much as any Formula 1 team on sportscar developments: the 904 was quickly followed by the spaceframe 906 six-cylinder 2-litre, the 907 eight-cylinder works racing cars, the 908 works and customer eight-cylinder cars, the ultra-light 909 hillclimb car, the 910 six- or eight-cylinder 2-litre, and ultimately the 917.

The objective was not just class wins, which Porsche had become rather good at over the past 15 years, but outright wins against the best opposition — Ferrari, Ford and Chaparral were the top teams of the 1960s, and Piëch meant to join them... and then beat them.

The modern generation: (1) The type 936 spyder and the type 935 coupé, both using turbocharged versions of the 911's six cylinder engine, won World Championships in both divisions in 1976 and again in 1977. (2) A stillborn project: Porsche's attempt to return to the single-seater world with a challenger for the Indianapolis 500 was thwarted by a last-minute change in the engine regulations. It never raced. (3) The 935 K3 (Kremer bodied) car with Britain's Brian Redman at the wheel at Le Mans. (4) The 924 Carrera GT with America's Al Holbert driving, also at Le Mans.

In 2-litre form and developing 210 horsepower, the flat-eight engine continued to give good service in sports cars throughout the 1960s; Porsche had repeated their outright victory of 1956, in the 1959 Targa Florio (Barth and Seidel in an RSK), and in 1960 (Bonner/Herrmann in an RS 60 development). The eight-cylinder engine took Bonnier/Abate to victory again in 1963, while in 1964 a new Porsche, the 904 GTS, scored a surprise win in Sicily handled by the English driver, Colin Davis, with Antonio Pucci. With five such victories behind them, Porsche had become the leading make at the Targa Florio; the team that was hardest to beat.

The type 904 was conceived as a customer car, a sturdy, all-purpose competitions car, which could run with a variety of four- or six-cylinder engines. Proving its versatility, the 904 followed up its Targa Florio win with a second place overall in the Monte Carlo Rally of 1965, when, in appalling weather conditions, Eugen Bohringer battled through to

It was the 908 model, with a completely new 3-litre engine developing 360 horsepower, that set Porsche off in the right direction. In 1968, honours were evenly shared with John Wyer's Ford GT40 team, and although Porsche scored more Championship points, Ford took the World Championship title by virtue of its five best scores. The following year, Porsche won seven races outright and clinched the World title easily, the only flaw in the programme being a narrow defeat at Le Mans.

On only its third outing, the type 917 had led easily at Le Mans, until put out by transmission failure, but this was the start of a new era for Porsche. It had a new flat-12 engine of 4.5 litre capacity, developing 550 horsepower initially, and was easily the most powerful sports car of its time. Still with a spaceframe tubular chassis, it was brutally fast, capable of achieving 220 miles per hour on the Mulsanne straight at Le Mans. The only problem was that Porsche had exhausted their budget

3

4

On the previous pages, a montage of Porsche success on the tracks. In the large picture, the fearsome 917/10 Can-Am and Interserie car with 800 brute horsepower. Inset, the 1971 Le Mans winning 917 trailed by a Ferrari 512; the 1981 Le Mans winning 936; Mark Donohue's Can-Am championship 917/30; the 936 and 935; the 1976 Le Mans winning 936; and the 944 on its debut outing at Le Mans where it finished seventh in 1981. On this page, the 935 in 1977 guise, and the Kremer bodied version. (Above) the East African Safari 911 which finished fourth in the 1978 event.

on the car's development, and for 1970 and 1971 the company entered into an agreement with John Wyer and his Gulf sponsors to race the car with full assistance from the factory. Ferrari replied with a 5-litre V12 cylinder model, the 512, which was equally effective on paper, but never realised it full potential.

It would be easier to list the races the Gulf-Porsches did not win in these two years, when Porsche easily secured the World Championship for Manufacturers twice in succession. Ironically John Wyer, the master tactician in long distance racing, did not win at Le Mans with the 917s; in

(3) *The first turbocharged 911 was a prototype racing car campaigned in 1974. Its success (second at Le Mans) accelerated production of the 911 Turbo model, and paved the way for the 936 (1) in its matt black prototype form. It was still black the first time it raced in 1976, but then reverted to white. (2) The powerful 935/78 won at Silverstone on its debut, faltered at Le Mans, and never raced again.*

1970 victory fell to the back-up 917 team of Porsche Austria, and in 1971 to the Martini-Porsche team. This was a golden era for Porsche, and for endurance racing as a category, and enthusiasts mourn the day when the controlling FIA changed the rules for 1972 and announced a 3-litre limit on long distance racing.

Porsche looked for new pastures, developing an open version of the 917 (917/10 for 1972, and 917/30 for 1973) for Can-Am racing in America. There, Roger Penske ran the team for Porsche and with the assistance of turbocharging, the Porsches became just as dominant as they had been on the World Championship trail previously. The 917/30 is probably the ultimate in sports cars, its 5.4 litre turbocharged 12 cylinder engine developing more than 1,100 horsepower, and with this weapon Mark Donohue became the Can-Am champion almost without challenge. But history has a habit of repeating itself, and at the end of 1973 the Can-Am organisers changed the rules and effectively banned the turbocharged cars with fuel consumption formula, so once again Porsche looked to Europe.

In 1973 Porsche had won the Targa Florio for the 11th and final time, with a 911 Carrera RSR driven by Gijs van Lennep and Herbert Müller. The narrow, bumpy Sicilian road course, lined with spectators and trees, was no longer considered safe for the latest generation of road racing machinery and the FIA cancelled its racing permit after the '73 event. One of the most difficult and spectacular races ever devised, it fell a victim to progress. The following year, with its Can-Am programme cancelled, Porsche applied turbocharging to the 911 Carrera and ran a small but effective programme, the best result being a second place at Le Mans.

For the 1976 season, the FIA had devised a new set of rules dubbed 'the silhouette formula', for it allowed almost unlimited modifications to production based cars, providing they still kept their original appearance. Taking the homologated 911 Turbo as their base, Porsche produced the Group 4 type 934 and the Group 5 (World Championship) type 935, and both cars were destined for outstanding successes in the next six seasons. The 934 was an almost sure Group 4 (Grand Touring) category

winner, and the 935 won the World Championship for Manufacturers in 1976, 1977, 1978 and again in 1979—in the latter year it was the outright winner at Le Mans, the first time for many years that a production car had won this event.

In a parallel programme, Porsche also developed the type 936 Group 6 car from the old 908, now using a 2.2 litre version of the production based flat six-cylinder engine. With around 600 horsepower in a light chassis, the 936 was ideal for the sportscar formula. It enabled Porsche to win outright at Le Mans in 1976 and in 1977, against fierce opposition from Renault (the tables were turned in 1978 when Renault narrowly beat Porsche), and once more in 1981, though using a 2.65 litre

development of this engine.

Porsche's run of Le Mans victories came comparatively late in the firm's competitions history, the first being in 1970, but five such wins in 12 attempts with cars capable of winning, is no mean feat.

This scant record of Porsche's 30 year competition history cannot possibly do justice to the countless hours of design, development and preparation that go into the success story, nor to the ingenuity, the improvisation, the cost or the toll it takes. It does, nevertheless, give some insight into the devotion that Porsche has for motor racing, and endurance racing in particular. It is a devotion which will almost certainly continue as long as Porsche make sports cars.

On the facing page, a beautiful example of the 904 and a customised 911 Turbo with 935 lookalike panels. Erwin and Manfred Kremer, the Cologne specialists, offer a spectacular K3 street car which is the ultimate in 911 road cars though it is not deemed necessary to tune the engine up. On this page, Bob Garretson's 1981 World Driver Championship 935 just off the track. The technical picture clearly shows the twin turbocharger system which takes the power up to 750 horsepower when required. Tack-on body panels disguise the true 911 ancestry of this version; the 935 won world championships from 1976 to 1979 inclusive, and won Le Mans outright in 1979 into the bargain.

Much of the work going on at Weissach is secret, and security at the centre is as tight as it would be at a military base. The small village in the Schwabian countryside west of Stuttgart is quite accustomed to seeing unusual vehicles purring through its narrow streets, heading for the Porschestrasse, which leads up the hill to Porsche's research and development centre. There, 1,000 scientists, technicians and engineers work on developments concerning not only their own company, but also much of the world's motor industry.

The research and development aspect is as old as Porsche's business, founded in 1931. The Volkswagen and the Auto-Union Grand Prix cars are two major projects that have been mentioned; the World War II Tiger tank, military versions of the Volkswagen, aero and military engines were other aspects between 1933 and 1945. The Cisitalia Grand Prix car, the 356 and all its successors were born on the team's drawing boards. A marvellous variety of racing cars, including the most powerful road racing car ever made, the 917/30 Can-Am model, were all developed at Weissach.

Yet much of the work will remain a secret for ever. Other manufacturers enjoy total confidentiality when they ask Porsche to design or develop new systems, and only the customer can ever break the secret. Outside publicity has been given to Porsche's work for

In 1982 Porsche again introduced a Cabriolet, this time on the 911 and the first to be offered since the 356C Cabriolet went out of production in 1965. The 911 Cabriolet, scheduled for production at the end of the year, has a folding top that is easy to use and features a zip-out rear window for additional ventilation and easy replacement. The 911 Cabriolet has a 204 horsepower version of the six cylinder engine, and weighs no more than other models in the 911 range. It is similar in construction to the Targa, but without the rollover hoop. No underfloor strengthening was found to be needed.

Volkswagen, Lada, Harley-Davidson, Chevrolet, Volvo, Alfa Romeo, and Ford of Europe to name a few, but this is merely lifting a corner of the carpet to take a look underneath. Ask a Porsche man the extent of the company's contract work for America, for instance, and he will say "Oh, two of the big three in Detroit". Which is saying quite a lot. The NATO Leopard tank was also developed in Weissach, and it would be reasonable to suppose that although Porsche is small in manufacturing terms, it is very big indeed as a consultancy. Two of Porsche's developments for the German government have been the SAVE and ORBIT systems, which are modules for dealing with emergency situations. The SAVE system consists of ambulance capsules which can be rushed to the scene of an accident or natural disaster, by road or air, enabling doctors to despatch the victims, with full medical care, to hospitals without delay; the ORBIT system is similar in concept, but is for firefighting.

The Weissach Research and Development Centre started off in the mid 1960s, initially with a circular skid pad in open country, where Porsche could test the handling and roadholding properties of their cars. Road circuits, which would make very nice racing tracks, were built around the skid pad, then came the buildings which house the engineers. By 1973 the Centre consisted of a new headquarters building of imposing design, where research is initiated, and two long main blocks of test houses.

These house mechanical workshops, woodworking shops, a foundry, heat treatment processing, plastics processing, prototype building shops, electron beam welding, fitting shops, climatic and anechoic rooms, dynamometers, crash facilities, seat belt test rigs, and many more facilities. Still unique, is a six-metre diameter drum used for tyre testing, novel in that the wheel and tyre run within the perimeter, rather than on the top surface. One of the advantages is that water can be retained instead of being thrown off, allowing better testing of the aquaplaning properties of a tyre.

The sound of cars running day and night attract the attention of the visitor. No drivers, just the cars. One or two models can be run on a constant cycle, day in, day out, on rolling roads for the American 50,000 mile emission test, without actually moving an inch. Robots in the passenger area operate the throttle and gearshifts quite automatically to a predetermined programme, and all these test rigs require is for someone to come along periodically to put more gasoline into the tanks. That's a task that even Porsche haven't mechanised yet.

Today, the Weissach facility occupies nearly half a million square metres of countryside, including 4.7 miles of test track, 1.2 miles of cross country torture for off-road and military vehicles (including Porsche's own rally cars), and pavé, washboard, 'ski jumps' and other fatigue inducing features.

Departments concentrate on project studies, technical system analyses and assessments, designs, calculations, styling, construction, testing, lightweight materials, air conditioning systems, a variety of internal combustion engines including Diesel, transmissions, brakes, new welding processes, light metal research, and armoured vehicle design. The list is almost endless, and it's true to say that Porsche will tackle almost any commission within its power.

It is surprising that time is found for racing, yet there is a comparatively small racing workshop, which draws visitors like a magnet. The same mechanics who work on future developments for Porsche and their customers, converge on the racing department when Le Mans, or another big race draws near, prepared to work night and day if necessary, to perfect the racing machinery. For Porsche, endurance racing is the biggest challenge, preferably with production based cars, and even the most sophisticated racing cars have to go through gruelling tests on the pavé and 'pancake' road to prove their strength. Anything that breaks here is unlikely to go the distance at Le Mans.

In the past few years the world has been through two major oil crises, and many people might find it difficult to imagine how a sports car manufacturer can pull through these times of hardship. Maybe the philosophy is a little different at Porsche, because they see the sports car as being an efficient, flexible machine which can very often pioneer techniques that bigger manufacturers will want to adopt later on. Windcheating, low-drag shapes have been of primary appeal to Porsche for 50 years or more, and today all the manufacturers follow suit; lighter weights with better materials, more efficient engine design, better handling, improved braking systems, all are things to be found in sports cars, and Porsches in particular.

Today, with 12,000 mile service intervals, seven year warranties on the galvanised chassis/ body units, aerodynamic body shapes, light weight, and sophisticated interior designs, Porsches do not conform to the old fashioned ideas of what a sports car should be. They do not have to be noisy, uncomfortable, draughty, heavy or harsh. Many women enjoy Porsche motoring, and men from all walks of life can get a thrill from the performance aspect without having to make big sacrifices in fuel consumption. Customers the world over will always seek something that is a little better, perhaps better made and rather more expensive than the norm, and as long as that holds true, there is a good future for Porsche.

(Overleaf) Wealthy German privateer Georg Loos driving his 917/10 through the Karussel at the Nurburgring, during an Interserie race in the mid-1970s. Loos, a building and property speculator, was Porsche's best customer for a time, running his own team of Interserie and World Championship cars including the 935, and helped to keep the World Championship for Makes in Stuttgart after the factory ceased to campaign in this division.

The publishers would like to offer their special thanks to Dr. Ing.h.c.
Porsche Aktiengesellschaft, Stuttgart-Zuffenhausen for allowing
photographic facilities at the factory, and to Porsche Cars Great Britain
Limited for the loan of current models.

Featuring the photography of Clive Friend FIIP and Nick Meers.
Research by Hanni Edmonds.

Acknowledgements

Picture Library Porsche., Stuttgart-Zuffenhausen.
London Art Technical Drawings Ltd.
Van Hallan—Photo-Features.

First English edition published by Colour Library International Ltd.
© 1982 Illustrations and text: Colour Library International Ltd., 99 Park Avenue, New York 10016
This edition is published by Crescent Books
Distributed by Crown Publishers, Inc.
h g f e d c b a
Colour separations by FER-CROM, Barcelona, Spain
Display and text filmsetting by Focus Photoset, London, England
Printed by Cayfosa and bound by Eurobinder - Barcelona (Spain)
Library of Congress Catalog Card No. 82-70291
CRESCENT 1982

Dep. Leg. B. 22.579/82